FACING the IMPOSSIBLE

A Father's Devotional of Loss, Love and Life

Adam Kornegay

ISBN 979-8-89345-201-3 (paperback)
ISBN 979-8-89345-202-0 (digital)

Copyright © 2024 by Adam Kornegay

All rights reserved. No part of this publication may be reproduced, distributed, or transmitted in any form or by any means, including photocopying, recording, or other electronic or mechanical methods without the prior written permission of the publisher. For permission requests, solicit the publisher via the address below.

Christian Faith Publishing
832 Park Avenue
Meadville, PA 16335
www.christianfaithpublishing.com

Printed in the United States of America

Dedicated to:

This Devotional is dedicated to my Lord and Savior, Jesus Christ, for always being my rock and for bringing me through one of the most challenging times of my life with such Peace and Joy.

To my sweet Haley, you filled our lives with many joyous memories that I cherish every day! I hear your laughter often and am reminded about the passion that you lived life!

To my wife, Kelly, who has always believed in me and supported me. Your support and strength mean more than you will ever know. Thank you for always encouraging me to be a better version of myself each and every day.

To Mikayla, the mountain that you have climbed wasn't always easy, but you have done it. There will be others but know that you are an inspiration for many people! Always stay true to you.

Finally, to all of my family and friends who lock arms with me to do life. This is truly a journey and my heart will forever be indebted to you.

Contents

Introduction vii

1. In That Moment 1
2. When All You Can Do Is Be Still 3
3. What About Those Logistics? — God Knows and Is Deeply Engaged 5
4. Wave After Wave of Emotion 7
5. Memories 9
6. Sharing Loss With Those Close to You 11
7. I Wish I had More Time – Did I Say All I Needed to Say 13
8. What About Faith – Is It Okay to Question God? 15
9. Look for Him – He is Everywhere 17
10. Be Aware of Inward Thinking Being All-Consuming – "My Pain" Above All Else 19
11. Here, There is Rest 21
12. Gifts From Loved Ones – Part 1 23
13. Gifts From Loved Ones – Part 2 26
14. He is LOVE Part 1 – How Much Does the Lord Love Us 28
15. He is LOVE Part 2 - What Has He Prepared For Us – Life is Finite To Us (We Are Born and We Die) – There is So Much More 30
16. Faith into Action – Where the Impossible Becomes Possible .. 32
17. Joy and Peace – Doesn't Always Mean Happiness 35
18. What now? – Living Each Day 37
19. Your New Journey Has Just Begun - Be Prepared and Intentional 39

20. Listen to His Voice – You Never Know What Will Be
    Coming Your Way 41
21. Walk With Your Father 43

Thought-Provoking and Encouraging Messages 45
Scripture Reference 67

Introduction

When we lose a loved one, it can often be one of the most difficult things that we have to deal with as humans. The raw emotion and sometimes actual physical pain that we go through can really mess with us. It can make us lose perspective, where nothing makes sense. Yet it is that perspective that we so desperately need during this time. Far too often, the messages that we hear or the well-intended support from some people leave us feeling void, and it is there that personal and professional relationships can crumble. I am here to tell you that it doesn't have to be that way. That the source of comfort can come from tapping into your faith and believing what God has already demonstrated by sending us His Son, so that we may not perish, but have everlasting life.

This devotional is intended for you to reflect, to bring you hope, to challenge you along the way, and ultimately bring you to a place of peace, the kind of peace that can only come from our Father. In these pages, I will share parts of my story when I lost my twenty-four-year-old precious daughter. My sincere hope is that through this, you will be able to see your relationship with our Father in a different, more powerful way. One which will ultimately lead you to genuine peace through the undeniable Love of our Lord and Savior Jesus, and receive His grace, His mercy, and His unfailing love, which knows no bounds.

The Bible is one major avenue that the Lord uses to speak to us. It is His blueprint, and contains the most amazing words ever written. It is Life. It is through the scriptures that we hang our hat on, that we lean into, and that we hold onto in faith. How do you know that the Bible can be trusted? Because it is the most accurate history book, without a mistake. People over time have had many theological discussions or disagreements about what was meant when He said certain things, but that doesn't discount the amazing precision that is held throughout the pages of His Word. There are over 63,700 cross-references (conceptional links that connects to scripture, dates, phrases, people, events, etc.) from both the Old and New Testament. God spoke through forty men to write His words over a period of 2,000 years on three continents and in three different languages. It is perfect. Lean into these words and trust them to be true. Not mine, but the Lord's. Let God speak to you, lead you, and comfort you in His words.

I believe wholeheartedly that God speaks to us in multiple ways—through the Holy Spirit, through the Bible, and through life's circumstances, to name a few. My prayer is that your relationship with God will be strengthened by reading His word, earnest prayer, and by committing to take action if it is placed on your heart.

This is a twenty-one-day devotional that is sincerely meant to grow your relationship with God, and perhaps a new perspective about how to face and deal with loss. I know that God certainly changed me through my journey. Each day you will be presented with a few scriptures to read and a devotion to think about. I would encourage you to go to God in prayer before starting and after you have finished reading. Then listen and consider what God is speaking into your heart. Think about starting a journal to capture your thoughts and emotions. Write down what God has done in your life or proclaim what He will do and watch Him work in your life.

Following the twenty-one days of devotion, I have written twenty-one inspirational, encouraging, or thought-provoking words to lead your mind and heart. These could be read at any time or left to the end as a mini devotion to carry you forward.

May you draw hope and inspiration through these pages. May you heal, strengthen, and find His true meaning in your life.

While much of this devotion is written through my experience with losing my daughter, I do believe that many of the lessons learned can be applied to any loss. Many of the emotions are similar. For example, if you have suddenly lost a job or you lost a home in a

FACING THE IMPOSSIBLE

fire, the emotional journey would be similar to that of losing a loved one. So, if you have suffered loss or even want to prepare yourself for the future, I encourage you to take this short journey with me, and may you experience peace that can only come from up above.

1

In That Moment

Psalm 34:18 – The LORD is near to those who have a broken heart, and saves such as have a contrite (crushed) spirit.

When we lose a loved one, it happens in a blink. Sometimes we know it is coming, but often it comes as a thief. When my daughter died, it had been sixteen days since I had last seen her, on a beautiful Christmas morning. Who would have known that it would be her last?

Her sobbing, controlled, yet guttural— "She's gone! Oh, Adam, I'm so sorry! She's gone!"

These are the words that rang in my head. These are the words my wife had just spoken to me. I had no air in my lungs, and a pain in my chest and stomach like I had never felt before. My mind spinning, trying to make sense of these words. How could this be?

I was guilty of taking this precious life for granted. Never in my wildest dreams did I ever even consider that I would outlive my daughter, yet it happened.

There were so many unanswered questions and numerous decisions that had to be made. To say that my mind and heart were spinning would be an understatement. All that I could do is cry out and pray. I knew that I needed God to help me navigate this. He knew that, too.

The mental spin and emotional roller-coaster is similar for us all. It is the end of the road for this relationship, this chapter of life. Now what?

Know this certainty: We are all His children, and He loves you beyond what you can hope or imagine. He knows the pain that you were or are in, and even if you feel that you are alone or the only one who feels that way, God is with you.

Reflection: The moment that you faced the loss of your loved one. What was that time was like for you? How did God meet you at that moment?

If you don't feel that He was there with you, or if you are struggling with God's existence because of your experience. I would encourage you to be honest, write down what you are feeling. Pray, even if you haven't prayed before, and continue reading.

Action: Capture your thoughts and write them down.

Matthew 5:4 – Blessed are those that mourn, for they shall be comforted.

Deuteronomy – 31:6 – Be strong and of good courage, do not fear nor be afraid of them; for the LORD your God, He is the One who goes with you. He will not leave you nor forsake you.

2

When All You Can Do Is Be Still

Psalm 46:10 – Be still and know that I am God.

The pain we feel when loss occurs is real and cannot be denied. Along with the physical pain and mental exhaustion, depending on the circumstances of your loss, there may be questions, confusion, and even anger. Sometimes nothing makes sense, yet the finality of it all is real. In this moment, breathing is a chore. Yet it happens, one breath at a time.

I believe that everyone can relate to this on some level. It is hard to describe the sudden vacuum inside. Emptiness—yet pain. Emptiness—yet heaviness and difficulty breathing. Emptiness—yet so much spinning inside. All we can do is go through the motions, and God knows that. He knows exactly what you are going through, even more than we can possibly understand. The Lord knows the pain because He watched a cruel world pass unjust judgment on His Son. He watched Jesus tormented, suffer through unimaginable pain and ultimately death. That price was paid for us so that we can have eternal life and a relationship with our Father, but even knowing the purpose, God had to watch this happen to his own flesh. He sees you and can relate with you.

Early on, when I was experiencing all of this pain, emotion and confusion, the Holy Spirit helped me to see God and encouraged me to trust Him and lean on Him. Looking back, it is amazing to see what my Father did when I found time to put the distractions aside and lay my pain at His feet. I sat there weeping and crying out to Him and when I couldn't do that anymore, I just sat with Him. It was then that peace and rest came to me.

The spectrum that we all go through varies from circumstance to circumstance, and our needs are also different. God formed you and made a way for you to be close to Him. There is intimacy in this. Let Him provide for you. Lean on Him and let Him be your comfort. He is more than big enough to handle all of your needs, questions, anger, sadness, emptiness, pain and exhaustion. His Love for you is so much more than you can know or even imagine. He will carry you through this. Be still.

Reflection: Praise God for loving us and drawing us close to Him so that we can find rest. Are you carrying pain and exhaustion with you? Consider if now is the time to trust God with what you have.

Action: Write down your thoughts and capture what God is saying to you. Pray and give thanks. He knows you and cares deeply.

Psalm 56:8 – You number my wanderings, put my tears into Your bottle. Are they not in Your book?
Isaiah 41:10 – Fear not, for I am with you. Be not dismayed, for I am your God. I will strengthen you, yes, I will help you, I will uphold you with My righteous right hand.

3

What About Those Logistics? — God Knows and Is Deeply Engaged

Philippians 4:19 – And my God shall supply all your need according to His riches in Glory by Christ Jesus.

As if all of the emotion wasn't enough, now the flood of logistics comes. Alongside loss, there is much to do. For me, this honestly was one of the hardest things that I had ever gone through. The unreal urgency and longing to be back with my family (I was 1,000 miles away at the time when I received the call from my wife) that I felt was almost palpable, which made it much more challenging to focus and manage this time that required me to make a myriad of decisions to get home.

In those early moments and days, while we are in a fog, we have calls and decisions to make, and details to put into motion. It is a lot to handle and I knew that is when I needed to turn it over to God. Pray and trust that He will help provide you with what you need to get through this time. It is easy to become consumed with it all. Resist it and watch His power at work around you. People may show up out of nowhere to offer assistance or provide relief. Circumstances may shift around you in special ways opening doors to help you navigate these times. A song or His word may pop up in an instant providing you comfort or peace just when you need it.

His mighty hand is navigating all of it—we just don't always take the time to recognize it.

I look back at the number of transportation details that had to be decided, people putting their lives on hold to show up, and family and friends out of nowhere that came to help. It was and is quite humbling, that He loves me that much to make it all happen. God was using all of them to help support us and provide us with what we needed at a time when our minds and hearts were at their weakest. There were moments, and I think many of us felt that way, that I didn't even have the mental capacity to know what to ask for. Like when the precious woman sitting next to me on one of my flights put down her book and lovingly allowed me to share pictures and talk about a few memories about my daughter. She stopped everything and I could tell she was praying and interceding for me. God knew that I needed someone in that moment as I was trying to get home. He knows you, and will show up in many ways.

Reflection: Looking back, what did God do for you? What logistics fell into place and how was God there for you, even if you didn't ask? If this is happening to you now or happened recently, ask the Lord to be with you now and be observant about His presence helping you through these times.

Action: Write it down what God has done or is doing for you. If you felt that you were abandoned at that time, cry out to Him now and let Him know how you feel. Write it down and give Him a chance to pour into your heart.

Philippians 4:13 – I can do all things through Christ who strengthens me.

Joshua 1:9 – Be strong and courageous. Do not be frightened, and do not be dismayed, for the LORD your God is with you wherever you go.

4

Wave After Wave of Emotion

Psalm 147:3 – He heals the brokenhearted and binds up their wounds.

Let's be honest, the pain is real, and emotions are raw. We are all uniquely different and react to mourning in different ways. Some people internalize everything, some open the floodgates, some lash out, some deflect, and others just clam up. Over time, people may experience several of these coping mechanisms. No matter how you deal with your emotions, the one thing that we all have in common is that it hits us in waves. At first, it is one right after another, and over time it spreads out.

I was probably in the floodgate column. Controlled, but the tears definitely poured. For me, it allowed momentary releases of pressure. Some of my triggers would have been a picture, someone saying something that reminded me of her, coming across a television program that she liked, or even just a fleeting memory. Any one of these could trigger emotions and, depending on where I was at or with what company I was in, those tears would pour. They aren't always sad tears either. I remember, on several occasions, some of my daughter's friends coming up to me and related stories about how much she meant to them. They told me about her loyalty and how much she would make them laugh. Each of those memories' made my eyes well up but not because I was sad, it was because I was so proud of the woman that she was.

There were also quiet times, usually in the evening, when I cried out asking God why. Why was she taken so early? Why now? I wanted someone to pay for this. I felt robbed of my time with her. All of these questions and emotions were leading me on a journey to something quite healthy, but in the early days, it was raw. I had to deal with my emotions and the very real loss of a beautiful twenty-four-year-old young woman.

No matter the circumstances surrounding your loss, the emotions are real, and God knows it too. He is intimately aware of the ups and downs that we feel and He wants to be our source of comfort. It is okay to question, let Him know you are mad, or just shed tears. He wants to be your Papa and hold you in His arms. Close your eyes and feel God's embrace.

Reflection: What was your journey like? How did you process, or how are you still processing the hurt?

Action: Pray and give it all to God. Don't hold back and be expectant to feel His presence.

Matthew 11:28 – Come to Me, all you who labor and are heavy laden, and I will give you rest.

2 Corinthians 1:3 – Blessed be the God and Father of our Lord Jesus Christ, the Father of mercies and God of all comfort

5

Memories

Proverbs 10:7 – The memory of the righteous is blessed ...

Memories. Good ones and bad ones, we all have them. They can be triggered in so many ways, and often, it doesn't take much. An emotion is oftentimes attached along with the memory. When they are good, we have happy tears, laugh, smile, or just sit in contentment. When they are not so good, we may have painful tears, sadness, lash out in anger, and sometimes physical pain. Our memories can lead our minds and hearts to make statements like: I just want more time; it should have been me; or this isn't fair. They can also bring on a roller-coaster of all the above. I remember one friend showing me a picture, which led to laughter. Then someone else made a comment that was sobering and then sadness came over us all. One moment up, the next down.

To be certain, the memories that we have are a compilation of special moments that tell a story. These are personal and perhaps one of the greatest gifts that we have. These memories are precious because they keep us connected to our loved ones until that special day when we see them again. There is so much comfort in believing that very truth.

For me, in the early days, the memories brought me happiness, then numerous questions and deep sadness. Yet as time went on (for me it was days), I could not escape the reoccurring thoughts that would not go away. I was being challenged. God was making it clear to me that I had a choice to make. I could choose to fixate on the sadness, or I could choose to fixate on the happiness. The choice was mine. If I simply dug in and allowed the heaviness to consume me, I would not have been good to anyone. My wife, older daughter, other family, and friends would all negatively pay a price. What God showed me is that the memories were a treasure trove that He placed in my mind that would bring me joy and peace, if I allowed it to. It became clear to me that I had to be intentional and choose to focus my mind and attention on the beautiful memories that brought a smile to my heart so I could be present and positive to those around me.

The joy also comes from another powerful memory. One that I didn't experience in person, but I did experience it through God's word. That is the memory of what Jesus did for us and how I know that God understands the pain of suffering, far more than anything that I could possibly imagine. With that memory, we know what love is!

Reflection: What are your memories?

Action: I would encourage you, no matter what is running through your mind today, to focus on that which is positive and make a choice to bring that to the forefront. You are not always able to control what triggers the memory, but you can control your response. Be intentional and see what God does in your heart.

John 3:16 – For God so loved the world that He gave His only begotten Son, that whoever believes in Him should not perish but have everlasting life.

Psalm 112:6 – Surely he will never be shaken. The righteous will be in everlasting remembrance

6

Sharing Loss With Those Close to You

Proverbs 17:17 - A friend loves at all times, and a brother is born for a time of adversity.

We are not meant to do life alone. Memories of our loved ones can sway us in radically different directions, depending on your experiences. It is easy to fall into a trap for some of us to think that they need to be alone in these times. I'm not speaking about moments of time when you need to get away and just "be" for a brief moment to collect yourself or just have some quiet time. I'm referring to isolation or pushing others away, and that is a place that we need to guard ourselves from. We aren't created to do life alone and God knows this.

God also wants to be at the center of this communion with you and your loved ones. He set the example when He called to His disciples to spend time with him before He left the earth. His ultimate sacrifice was the supreme example of love and desire to commune with us. He laid down His life so that we would not be apart.

Keeping God at the center and surrounding ourselves with people can have a very positive impact on us. When we share what is deep in our hearts with others, it can decompress what is building up on the inside, perhaps leading to a bit more sleep. It can allow others to step up and help carry our burdens. Sharing not only blesses us, but it keeps our loved one's memory alive.

Hearing what other people have to say can be incredibly heartwarming and provide even more fuel for you to focus on that which is positive. There is so much to say about doing life together in a community. There really aren't hard rules when it comes to spending time alone or together. I believe, like with just about everything, there is a balance. Embrace your community and be open to them.

Reflection: Think about your time sharing with others.

Action: Capture the moments and write them down. If you were one of the people who withdrew, consider changing that today and reaching out to God and your community. See the power in it.

Galatians 6:2 – Bear one another's burdens, and so fulfill the law of Christ.

Ecclesiastes 4:9-12 - Two are better than one, because they have a good return for their labor: If either of them falls down, one can help the other up. But pity anyone who falls and has no one to help them up. Also, if two lie down together, they will keep warm. But how can one keep warm alone? Though one may be overpowered, two can defend themselves. A cord of three strands is not quickly broken.

7

I Wish I had More Time – Did I Say All I Needed to Say

Romans 8:18 – For I consider that the sufferings of this present time are not worthy to be compared with the glory which shall be revealed in us.

Whether we have lost our loved one unexpectedly or we knew it was coming, oftentimes we still wish that we had more time with them, and we often ask ourselves, "Did I say all that I needed to say?"

For me, my daughter's death was a sudden loss, and, along with the "whys," I immediately craved more time with her. I had seen her just three weeks prior, on Christmas Day. It was a precious, joyous time filled with laughter and great food. But I fell into the trap of taking it for granted that I would see her again, sometime soon. When that didn't happen, of course, I felt robbed. I had run the gamut of emotions and thoughts, but this is truly where God began to work on my heart and lay the foundation of true peace that comes from His word and promises.

I have heard it said so many times from friends: "I wish I had said …" fill in the blank. This can be haunting for some people who are running the marathons of life from one experience to the next without necessarily slowing down and considering: Am I fostering all that I can in my relationships? While this may be a revelation that affects our existing relationships moving forward, what about the ones that we lost? Absent of the promises from God there could be a void in your heart.

It is completely normal to desire more time. We just can't get stuck. This is the time to really trust God and His word. What do you believe, and can you turn it over to Him? Rest on the understanding that, through Him, we will be joined together and reunited.

Reflection: Think about God's promises and what they mean to you. Let this seep deep into your heart, because these truths are paramount to finding true peace and joy that come from our most loving Father.

Action: Make sure that you have said all that you want to say to all of those people close to you in life.

John 16:22 – Therefore you now have sorrow; but I will see you again and your heart will rejoice, and your joy no one will take from you.

Rev 21:4 – And God will wipe away every tear from their eyes; there shall be no more death, nor sorrow, nor crying. There shall be no more pain, for the former things have passed away.

8

What About Faith – Is It Okay to Question God?

Hebrews 4:16 – Let us therefore come boldly to throne of grace, that we may obtain mercy and find grace to help in time of need.

This may be obvious to some but not as obvious to others. It is *not* wrong to question God. In fact, quite the opposite. He wants us to question Him, spend time with Him, and realize our uttermost dependence on Him. Through this process of questioning and spending time, we come to understand that His ways are not always our ways. That His love and desire for goodness in our lives far outreaches the boundaries and capacity of our minds and hearts.

After my loss, I found myself questioning everything. This was part of my healing process, but it was time for me to begin this reckoning within myself. Do I believe what I think that I believe and is God who He says that He is? Due to how my daughter passed away, I wanted justice, but justice isn't mine to pass. I wanted peace and was all tied up inside. I wanted to lead my family, but I was stumbling. I wanted my daughter back, but the time to see her again would have to wait. I had to go through the process.

Questioning God is healthy and very normal in times of loss. The pressure cooker of life, combined with our finite minds, actually requires this of us. This is where we continue our journey of understanding and ultimate acceptance.

Eventually, the questions can subside, and you can submit to His Truth, and trust is cemented.

Reflection: Be honest with yourself and ponder the questions that you have or had and where did they lead you. Did they lead you closer to God or did you choose to hold on too tightly?

Action: If they led you closer, praise Him. If they didn't, and you are still holding on to unanswered questions, now is the time to release those feelings and submit to His promises. Spend time with God. Your faith will release something special in you which either has or will allow you to become a better version of yourself, better suited to serve your family moving forward.

John 20:29 - Because you have seen Me, you have believed. Blessed are those who have not seen and yet have believed.

Romans 5:1-5 – Therefore, having been justified by faith, we have peace with God through our Lord Jesus Christ, through whom also we have access by faith into this grace in which we stand, and rejoice in hope of the glory of God. And not only that, but we also glory in tribulations, knowing that tribulation produces perseverance; and perseverance, character; and character, hope. Now hope does not disappoint, because the love of God has been poured out into our hearts by the Holy Spirit who was given to us.

9

Look for Him – He is Everywhere

Joshua 1:9 – Be strong and courageous. Do not be frightened, and do not be dismayed, for the LORD your God is with you wherever you go.

When we lose a loved one, especially when it is unexpected, the world seems to be going at an incredible pace, and it is difficult to keep up. Logistics, decisions, people, money, one thing after another. Combine all that with our human emotions, and it becomes quite easy to miss the work of our God in our circumstance. We know that we are to look to our Father always, but it is easy to get all wrapped up in ourselves or in what is happening around us. It is hard to slow things down and see that God is truly at work.

He loves us with such intensity that He has promised us that He will not leave us or forsake us. His word doesn't say that He "might" be with you, it says that He "will" be with you. All we have to do is look away from ourselves for a moment and seek our loving Father. I was praying one morning and it was as if a veil was lifted from my mind. Many things that were just chaotic suddenly became clearer. I was able to see so many connections to God in my circumstances and an incredible peace came over me. His work truly is all around us, even when we aren't looking for it.

When we turn our heads up to our Father, something magical happens. Not only does something beautiful happen inside of us at that moment, but we are also able to see His mighty hand at work.

That is not hyperbole, it is real. It doesn't change the facts surrounding loss or anything else, but our perspective changes.

God speaks to us through His word, using other people and our circumstances. Our Father cares deeply about each one of us. We may not always understand the "whys," and maybe that is okay in this moment.

Reflection: How many ways has God worked greatness in your life, even during heavy times? He was there and always will be. If you didn't see Him during those times, ask Him to show you now.

Action: Write in your journal what God has done.

Psalm 29:11 – The LORD will give strength to His people; The LORD will bless His people with peace.

Deuteronomy 31:8 – And the LORD, He is the One who goes before you. He will be with you, He will not leave you nor forsake you; do not fear nor be dismayed.

10

Be Aware of Inward Thinking Being All-Consuming – "My Pain" Above All Else

Romans 12:2 – And do not be conformed to this world, but be transformed by the renewing of your mind, that you may prove what is good and acceptable and perfect will of God.

When we are facing moments of such intense emotion, it is easy to fall into a trap of being consumed with the pain and hurt that we feel. This consumption, while understandable, can prevent us from seeing the truth and majesty all around us. It can also hinder relationships or even blessings that were meant for us.

If you find yourself in the prison of not being able to move forward after a sudden tragedy, consider a couple of things. What can you add to your life by remaining in active grief, and what can you offer your family and friends? You alone control this. I believe that there are forces that want to keep us stuck, but God will set you free.

I was definitely struggling but I had this pull inside my mind and really felt that I needed to dig deep. I knew that if I allowed the pain that I felt to consume me, and not give it up to my Father, that it would have been all that I would think about. I would have been an absolute mess and no good to my family or anyone. There were times that I wanted to push everyone away from me, and just crawl in bed. I believe that the Holy Spirit knew that about me and gently nudged and empowered me to act differently.

You see, whether or not we are aware, God is with us. There is nothing, absolutely nothing, that you feel that He has not felt Himself. Because of that, He knows of your pain, your hurt, and wants you to give it to Him. He is big enough, and through the action of accepting our pain, He will unleash a Peace over you that will go far beyond our understanding.

I felt that if I made this tragedy about me, my hurt, and my pain, what would that say about what I truly believe? What about my surviving daughters' pain? What about my wife's pain? What would that say about what I believe in scripture? Is God who He says that He is? Was I going to believe the lie that He is true to His word … except in this situation? Deep down, I knew the truth, and God was moving in my life in a powerful way. These questions were the ones that propelled me to pray and seek answers. I didn't always get the answer I wanted, or an answer at all but I did make firm faith choices to believe and those choices changed my life forever.

So, as I acted in obedience to Him, faithfully giving the hurt to Him, I was slowly freed enough that it allowed me to a) be a blessing to my family through strength, and b) see the undeniable truth that God was loving me through so many others. This strengthened me, and, through faith, I was able to see God act.

Reflection: Reflect on how you were or are dealing with your pain. What did you do with it?

Action: If you are still holding on to the pain, I would encourage you that now is the time to release it to God. It isn't too late. Watch Him at work within you and all around you.

Philippians 4:7 – The Peace of God, which transcends all understanding, will guard your hearts and minds in Christ Jesus.

Hebrews 4:15,16 – For we do not have a High Priest who cannot sympathize with our weakness, but was in all points tempted as we are, yet without sin. Let us therefore come boldly to the throne of grace, that we may obtain mercy and find grace to help in time of need.

11

Here, There is Rest

Psalm 4:8 – I will both lie down in peace, and sleep; For You alone, O LORD, make me dwell in safety.

Sometimes, we just need rest. Rest for the body. Rest for the mind. Rest for the soul. It can come with a good night's slumber, and it can also happen in short bursts throughout the day.

No matter how it comes, we need it, and the real source is given by God. Our brains go a thousand miles, consumed with our own business, hurts and sufferings. We have our lists, "to-do's" and if there is space in our head, we try to take care of others. Simply put, we are saturated and apart from bringing in our Father, we really can't know rest because there isn't anything to do with what is on our minds. God wants it all.

I can remember times sitting in my living room, just completely saturated and spent. My mind had just been bouncing between grieving, logistics and taking care of the people around me. I was reaching an end because I wasn't giving it up to God. I was holding on and what I really needed was rest. Without fail, something was put in my mind and heart that would remind me that it is okay to just "be" and sit with God. In those moments, I didn't have to be anyone to someone or do anything, I could just "be" and rest. It wasn't isolation for any really long period of time, but a few moments where I could quiet my mind and specifically give each thing to my Father. Then, I would find myself drifting off for a short nap, or other times I would just zone out, but real rest is what I received. Even in those bursts of time, I would stir up feeling more refreshed and with some clarity. All I know is that I felt different, in a really positive way.

God is consistently seeking after our hearts and time with us. This is why rest is so meaningful to Him and why it truly only comes when you lean into your Father. He wants us to rely on him. What loving father doesn't want to give comfort and replenish a broken heart?

Reflection: Reflect on the moments when you truly allowed yourself to be still and lean into God. What happened?

Action: Remind yourself of the loving gift of rest and what it empowered you to do. If you are still holding on all of your emotions and lists, maybe now is the time for you to take that step, close your eyes, and truly give in. Praise God for coming to us and meeting us right where we are.

Jeremiah 31:25 – For I have satiated the weary soul, and I have replenished every sorrowful soul.

Matthew 11:28-30 – Come to Me, all you who labor and are heavy laden, and I will give you rest. Take My yoke upon you and learn from Me, for I am gentle and lowly in heart, and you will find rest for your souls. For My yoke is easy and My burden is light.

12

Gifts From Loved Ones – Part 1

Matthew 22:37-40 – Jesus said to him, "You shall love the LORD your God with all your heart, with all your soul, and with all your mind. This is the first and great commandment. And the second is like it: You shall love your neighbor as yourself. On these two commandments hang all the Law and the Prophets."

We know that the greatest commandment is to love our Father with all of our heart, mind, and soul. His second commandment follows, and it charges us to love our neighbor, just as we love ourselves. The charge for us to love our neighbor and even our enemy is written many times throughout scripture. I know that we have tried very hard during our life to be givers and love those around us. It truly has been our honor and privilege to pour out our hearts and love on others during their times of need. Now, this was our time to be on the receiving end.

God knows that not only are we to love, but we are to be loved. After we experience a loss, we need people. Even if you are one of those people who push others away, if you are being honest, you really want them around. That is how we are created. We crave people and to have our brokenness held up by people that we can trust to love us, just as we are. These people with sit with us, pray with us, cry with us or even do tasks for us. Whatever it is, they are doing it out of love and support for you, and if you are being honest, it is exactly what we need.

My wife's sister and brother-in-law dropped everything and drove 1,000 miles immediately to be with us, without question. Other relatives did the same, coming in from even greater distances. Everything was so fresh and overwhelming, that in the early moments, we didn't even think to ask—they just responded to what God put on their heart. They came to provide support, helped take care of logistics, sit with us, cry with us, and be our crutches. Just what we needed and yet didn't even know that is what we needed. Yet, God knew. Words yet again can't truly describe what their selflessness meant.

They weren't alone. Family members from across the country, friends from all over, and neighbors dropped what they were doing in life to come and pour out their love to us. It was honestly, unbelievably humbling, and yet beyond special. If I am being honest, maybe I didn't feel worthy of it. Deep down, every one of those interactions was needed to help us get through. God was loving us through each person, and we felt it.

Reflection: What was your experience when people came to you wanting to support you? Who dropped what they were doing to show you how much they love you? To be there for you, during what may have been one of the most difficult times in your life, and hold you up. Write down each person and what they meant to you. Consider reaching out to them to let them know just how much they meant to you during that time.

If you are one of those people who had difficulty inviting others to be with you in your time of grief, it is okay. Perhaps consider thinking about why you were in that place, and who you would have liked to have been there.

Action: Reach out to those who impacted you and let them know how special they are.

If they weren't there and you realize that you should have invited them to help you, consider reaching out to them and simply let them know. My guess is that even though they weren't with you physically, they were emotionally and were praying for you.

Consider sharing, mentoring and being with someone who is having difficulty receiving the love that God pours thorough those around you.

John 15:12-13 – This is my commandment, that you love one another as I have loved you. Greater love has no one than this, than to lay down' one's life for his friends.
Romans 12:10 – Be devoted to one another in love. Honor one another above yourselves.

13

Gifts From Loved Ones – Part 2

Ephesians 2:10 – For we are God's handiwork, created in Christ Jesus to do good works, which God prepared in advance for us to do

When you go through a loss, isn't it amazing the people that come into your life? Family, friends, co-workers, people that you may not have gotten along with, and even some strangers to you, all suddenly show up. They show up to pour out their hearts, offer comfort and many come with offerings. I was blown away by the generosity and care of so many people who wanted to express love in so many ways. Sometimes it came in the form of a frozen lasagna or cooler of water, the music of a chime or a personal memento, and many bouquets of flowers.

People want to help, to communicate that they care, but, depending on their relationship with you, they might not always know how. Sending mom's best baked ziti recipe just seems like the perfect way to help. Right? So, you end up getting a lot of this at a time when your energy level is probably low and your mind is on a thousand other things.

Along with several members of our family, we had very dear friends who put a pause on their lives just to come and help organize the many offerings of love that were flowing our way. Wow, was that incredibly thoughtful. The food and drinks came in so useful to feed visitors and even sustain us a bit after everyone went home. It was great that we didn't have to think about what meal to cook or where to put things. We could just trust that these logistics were being handled. What a blessing.

So was also very humbling. Our lives were so consumed with doing life that I don't think I every really paused long enough to truly reflect how many lives that we had touched over the years. Here they were to give back. We were and forever will be eternally grateful and thankful for each of these family members and friends for their gestures and generosities.

Reflection: Reflect on all the wonderful gestures that were given to you and who gave them. Each one was a measure of love that was sent from people God used to show you that He will provide. Consider sending them a letter of gratitude to let them know how much it meant to you.

Action: Most importantly, stop, pray, and thank God for putting them in your life.

Romans 12:13 – Share with the Lord's people who are in need. Practice hospitality.

Proverbs 11:25 – A generous person will prosper; whoever refreshes others will be refreshed.

14

He is LOVE Part 1 – How Much Does the Lord Love Us

1 John 4:16 – And we have known and believed the love that God has for us. God is love, and he who abides in love abides in God, and God in him.

God loves you! More than your mind and heart can possibly truly understand. His love is mighty. His love is genuine. His love is real and deep.

Stop and consider the life of Jesus. A perfect man on earth, sent by His Father, as a sacrifice for … you. Personalize that. Insert your name. God knew that we would not be able to atone for our sins, so He paved a way for us and laid down His life, so that we may live.

Depending on the circumstances of your loss, there can be an emptiness, deep sadness, or even anger. God knows all of the emotions on the spectrum, so go ahead and share them with Him. Let Him have it and build on your relationship with Him. There isn't a feeling that you have that He doesn't know. Let that wash over you, and let the warmth of His love rise from within. He does not want to be apart from you. That is how much He loves us.

Reflection: Reflect and consider the true life, moments leading to the cross, death, and resurrection of Jesus Christ. What did He really endure, his unimaginable sufferings done for us in love, so that we would never be separated from the Father? Absolute LOVE!

Action: If you have not done so, consider giving or rededicating your life to Jesus. Let Him wash over you in a precious and special way.

1 John 4:9-11 – In this the love of God was manifested toward us, that God has sent His only begotten Son into the world, that we might live through Him. In this is love, not that we loved God, but that He loved us and send His Son to be the propitiation for our sins. Beloved, if God so loved us, we also ought to love one another.
John 15:13 – Greater love has no one than this, than to lay down one's life for his friends.

15

He is LOVE Part 2 - What Has He Prepared For Us – Life is Finite To Us (We Are Born and We Die) – There is So Much More

John 14:2 – In My Father's house are many mansions; if it were not so, I would have told you. I go to prepare a place for you.

As humans, our brains are often wired to see black and white. Beginnings and endings. Therefore, life can seem very finite to us. We see life come into the world through birth, a time to celebrate all things new. Then we pass on, leaving a void for those left behind. It is dramatic on both spectrums. One is generally associated with happy and joyous feelings, and the other is generally associated with heaviness and sadness. This is what we see and what we feel. A beginning and an end. Yet, there is so much more.

I've probably said it a hundred times over the years to friends who have lost loved ones: "You will see them again," "They are in heaven," and, "They aren't suffering anymore." On and on, one comment is similar to another. All of them, sincerely from my heart, and meant to provide some degree of comfort. I was speaking the truth, even if I hadn't let those concepts fully penetrate into my full conscious. When I lost my daughter, it was time for real understanding to take root.

God demonstrates His love in so many ways while we are on this planet, but truth be told, He isn't in this for the short game. He wants our hearts now and always. This is why Jesus went to the cross for us. So that we would have eternal life! Rest on that: eternal life. That doesn't resonate with our human mind, which says that there is a beginning and an end. Eternity is different and can be hard to wrap our heads around. It means that life *will* go on, beyond our comprehension.

Imagine that you have company coming over to your house. What do you do? You go through your list of things to check off to prepare for their arrival. You take time to do extra cleaning and put fine touches all over to make them feel welcome. Maybe you purchase special soaps or food items so that they will feel special. Well, that is exactly what God is doing for us in Heaven. He loves us so much that He has prepared a place for us. Imagine all of the special details that He has put into it.

There is more than a beginning and an end to life.

Reflection: Reflect about what His mighty love has in store for you. If you do many things for the arrival of your guest, imagine how much more He will do for you. God has prepared something truly magical.

Action: If you have already accepted this truth and are "all-in" for the majesty that He has created for us, praise him in prayer and song. If you are still wrestling with this, pray and ask God to reveal the truth to you. Let the Holy Spirit move inside of you.

John 16:33 – I have said these things to you, that in me you may have peace. In the world you will have tribulation. But take heart; I have overcome the world.

1 Thessalonians 4:13-14 But I do not want you to be ignorant, brethren, concerning those who have fallen asleep, least you sorrow as others who have no hope. For if we believe that Jesus died and rose again, even so God will bring with Him those who sleep in Jesus.

16

Faith into Action – Where the Impossible Becomes Possible

2 Corinthians 5:7 – For we walk by faith, not by sight.

These last couple of weeks have all led to this question: What do we really believe?

I was on a journey to make sense of my personal tragedy. All roads led to my human mind and heart not being capable of this kind of understanding. If I hadn't had my faith in God, there was no way that I could. So, I leaned in through prayer and had an openness for the Holy Spirit to show me truth. Doing so made me question what I really believed about His love and care for us. For me? I had to personalize it. It wasn't about "us" at this point, it was about "me" and what I believed about His love. I couldn't just go through the motions or act a part in church. What did I really believe about His love and care for me and my family? We have referenced the past couple of days (and really only scratched the surface) how much and how deep God's love is for us. If it is really true, and He says that it is, then what?

I know in my heart how crazy in love I am with my family. There isn't anything that I wouldn't do for them. I would have done almost anything for my daughter. I'm sure that you can relate. You know how much and how deeply you love those close to you. You would do anything to keep them safe, provide for them, and give them a place for belonging—no matter what. Even as flawed people, we know deep inside that the love that we have for our family, and as great as it is, pales in comparison to the love that the Lord our Father has for us. That is a simple statement to make, yet it blew my mind when I had a heart connection to that fact. My Father's love for me cannot compare with the love that I shower on my family. Honestly, my mind is still probably not fully capable of really understanding the true depths of that Love, but I try. He loves us infinitely more than we can know or even imagine. How powerful!

Here is where it gets interesting. I know without a shadow of a doubt how much I love my daughter. How much you love your loved ones. If we really believe, even if we can't fully wrap our minds around it, that the Lord is crazy about us and loves us deeply, how can we be upset? Yes, we will grieve, but this is our opportunity to free ourselves from the real pain, because we can now find joy in that our loved ones are in His loving arms. They aren't dealing with daily stress, financial woes, sickness, or strife in any way. My daughter, like your loved one, is free from all of that.

This is where faith turns to action. This is where we are tested. This is where the rubber meets the road.

Of course, I miss her. You will miss your loved one. Our human minds still work within the framework of finite beginnings and endings. But it is here that our faith in the Lord and His promises tells us that there is so much more! We **will** be united again. I will see my daughter again. You will see your loved one again. Through that belief, and knowing the depth of His Love, I believe that is where we can celebrate and turn the deep pain into something different. This is something that we can control where we want our minds and hearts to go. We can choose to ignore that fact and allow the pain to engulf us, or we can shout out praises to God for his love that He has demonstrated and will continue in so many ways.

This understanding is impossible to settle on our own, yet with God, the impossible becomes possible. God can turn that heaviness and sadness or even anger into something that is more joyous and positive. Declare His goodness and Love, walk in those truths, and watch what the Holy Spirit will do to your heart. Put Him to the test and watch as His love falls upon you in a special way. I spoke truth to this, and I found undeniable Peace. You will also.

Reflection: Reflect on where you were and where you are now with your faith. What was once impossible that you now see as possible?

Action: Pray and make a decision to put what you believe in your mind, into your heart. Give God all the glory!

Matthew 19:26 – But Jesus looked at them and said to them, "With men this is impossible, but with God all things are possible."

James 2:18 – But someone will say, "You have faith, and I have works." Show me your faith without your works, and I will show you my faith by my works.

17

Joy and Peace – Doesn't Always Mean Happiness

John 16:22 – So with you: Now is your time of grief, but I will see you again and you will rejoice, and no one will take away your joy.

As humans, we are conditioned to believe and think that joy and peace are always associated with being happy, having pleasurable feelings, or being free of conflict. While that can be true, it is honestly a pale way of genuinely looking at what joy and peace really are.

True joy comes from tapping into God and can only happen by having a relationship with Him. It is completely transformative and can change the hardest of times into a feeling of being blessed. It can take absolute heartache and turn it into gratitude—a place within ourselves that we come from when we are dealing with loss. We see examples of this throughout the world. People who have little or had much taken from them still feel blessed for what they have because He is the source of it. Apart from Him, there is no true anything.

That is the key. He is the source, and we make the choice to walk with him. Feeling blessed and grateful comes from a place that is not anchored in the self. It can't be. Because of that, we are able to bring our difficulties, struggles, and our loss to our Father, put them at His feet, and allow His goodness to wash over us.

Similar to joy, having a peaceful feeling is very different from having true peace. Generally speaking, peace is the absence of conflict between people. Like with true joy, true peace can really only come from our love of God, because it ushers us into a place of wholeness, and we are completely fulfilled.

These are incredibly important points to bring to the surface during a time of significant loss. Making a choice to fully believe what God has written into His word, and then apply it to our lives, allows this feeling of true joy and peace to wash over us, even when we ache. It won't make sense immediately, yet it will when we put it into action. We may not be happy, but we will be content, whole, blessed, and grateful. That's something that the world alone can't offer.

Allow Him to change your perspective about what joy and peace really are.

Reflection: Reflect about what you may have thought about joy and peace. Allow Him to move you into completeness and discern what the world would have you believe and what He wants you to see.

Action: Pray and ask God to help you see beyond your current understanding. Write this down in your journal.

John 15:11 – These things I have spoken to you, that My joy may remain in you, and that your joy may be full.

Philippians 4:7 – And the peace of God, which surpasses all understanding, will guard your hearts and your minds in Christ Jesus.

18

What now? – Living Each Day

Proverbs 3:5-6 – Trust in the LORD with all your heart, and lean not on your own understanding; in all your ways acknowledge Him, and He shall direct your paths.

Throughout scripture, the Lord uses definitive words and statements like "I will," "I have," "In all," and "with all." These are powerful, yet do we really believe them? I, for one, was really challenged by this after losing my daughter.

If He "will" see us again, and "all" things really work for the good, then what should my response be to those truths? This is when a light switch was flipped in my heart. Instead of focusing on what I had lost and the pain that was associated with it, I started choosing to really believe in His word. If they are true, then I don't need to be consumed with sadness, because I know I will see her again. I know that, somehow, there is a purpose in what happened to her. Why? Because His word says so.

Our hurts, confusion, anger, or heaviness can consume us if we don't lean in and really accept the words "will" and "all" in our lives. We can choose to hold on to our difficult feelings, or we can release them back to the Lord and lean into His promises, even when it doesn't always make sense in our minds or hearts. These really aren't just "feel good" words, they are real promises from our Father. They are something that we can truly trust. Our Lord and Savior loves us infinitely more than we can ever imagine. He will fulfill what He says that He will.

Acceptance of these precious promises is the key, because it gives us hope and ushers in true peace. If "all" things really do work for the good and He "will" see us again, then I don't have to understand the whys of my loss, I can move to believe the truth and just submit to His glory.

The waves of sorrow do get further apart, but they still come, and that is okay. I miss my daughter every day. But when I do, after some time of reflection and missing her, I always smile. I know that she is safe and in the loving hands of my Father and Savior Jesus! How could a loving father want anything more for his child?

All your ways, Lord, in all things …

Reflection: Reflect about how you feel about his "all" and "will" promises in scripture. Have you leaned into those promises or have you held back? Do you believe them? Do they lighten your burdens?

Action: If you have held back, I encourage you to release what you have been holding on to and receive all of those promises meant for you.

Matthew 6:34 – Therefore do not worry about tomorrow, for tomorrow will worry about its own things. Sufficient for the day is its own trouble.

Romans 8:28 – We know that all things work together for good to those who love God, to those who are called according to His purpose

19

Your New Journey Has Just Begun - Be Prepared and Intentional

Proverbs 2:6-8 — He plans success for the decent and honorable; he guards the course and protects the way of his faithful ones.

There were and are plenty of moments when emotions completely consume your mind and heart. It is challenging sometimes to always remember to just turn it over, and our Father knows that.

Making new choices isn't always easy. I believe that there is both spiritual goodness and evil in this world. A study for another time. The bible talks about the dark forces and that they do not want you or me to have peace and joy in any circumstance. Because of that, I knew that I needed to start my day and walk through it differently. I needed to be intentional about my actions, what I was reading, who I was surrounding myself with, and consistently turn to God when the hurts tried to pull me away.

Any time we want to create new habits, depending on the study that you read, it can take between two and three months for that new behavior to become more automatic. So, it really does take a measure of intentionality to rewire the brain and heart to react in the manner in which you desire.

I started doing daily prayers first thing in the morning. This was something that I had started to do but wasn't consistent with it. During my quiet time, I also did my best to not put my requests first, but to be grateful and thankful to the Lord for His love and faithfulness to me. Starting with gratitude and thankfulness seemed to bring my heart immediately into a different place, which had a calming effect on my mind and heart.

I believe that it is also very important to be generous to others. Generosity is something that further takes our mind off of the pain that we are feeling, and gives purpose and life. It isn't always easy to think about giving to other people at this time, but it can be done, even in small ways. I remember going through my daughter's "things" and as we found certain items, we knew that we needed to give them to friends or family members. There was such an amazing connection in those actions.

Finally, it is important to rest when you need to rest. Previously discussed, yet worth re-mentioning. You need it, and God knows that.

It is a balancing act to try and hone in on new, positive habits that lead us to have joy and peace. Sometimes we get it right, and other times we don't. But remember to run the race with endurance and know that He loves you and is always there for you. Be intentional.

Reflection: Think about what new steps you can take in your prayer life and throughout your days that will be meaningful to you. What can you do when that heavy memory hits to instead lean in and trust in His word, allowing a transformation to happen within you?

Action: Prepare your mind and heart. How do you want to do things differently and be intentional about it.

Psalm 9:1 – I will give thanks to the Lord with my whole heart; I will recount all of your wonderful deeds.

Matthew 6:33 – But seek first the kingdom of God and his righteousness, and all these things will be added to you.

20

Listen to His Voice – You Never Know What Will Be Coming Your Way

Psalm 144:1 – Blessed be the LORD my Rock, Who trains my hands for war, and my fingers for battle – My lovingkindness and my fortress, my high tower and my deliverer, My shield and the One in whom I take refuge, Who subdues my people under me.

God loves you so much that He wants to fight your fight and move the mountains that He knows that you cannot do on your own!

Have you ever had a time when you responded to something that you believe was from God, and it impacted you in a way that you couldn't possibly have imagined? This is exactly what happened to my wife and me.

It was one year and nine days before our daughter passed away that we both had it on our hearts to stop being Christers (going to church on Christmas and Easter) and to attend church every week. Every year, my wife and I go to a specific location to review the past year and create a bucket list for the new year. This is a tradition for us, where we reflect on the past and dream about our future as individuals and as a couple. At this particular meeting, it was so clear to us that we needed to attend and become part of the church.

Throughout the next year, we would be loyal in attending. Our faith grew, new habits were formed, and we did our best to keep God at the center of all that we did. Little did we know at the time that by listening to His voice on that January morning, He would be preparing us to handle the most traumatic event in our lives only one year and nine days later.

The journey that we both went on after the tragedy was one that drew us even closer together. Why? Because we had God at the center of everything we did. Our journey through grief wasn't made up of my actions or that of my wife's, but it was God that held us together. Had we not listened to His voice that morning and laid a strong foundation of faith, I shudder to think about what would have happened.

You see, God was fighting this battle long before I even knew that there would be one. I just needed to respond to his call.

Reflection: What has God put on your heart? Have you listened? Reflect about what that may have been, and if you didn't listen, consider making a different choice. If you did, praise Him for it. May it make you smile, as it did me.

Action: Let this be part of your story and share it with others.

Revelation 3:20 – Behold, I stand at the door and knock. If anyone hears my voice and opens the door, I will come into him and eat with him, and he with me.

Psalm 31:7 – I will be glad and rejoice in Your unfailing love, for You have seen my troubles, and You care about the anguish of my soul.

21

Walk With Your Father

Joshua 1:9 – Be strong and courageous. Do not be frightened, and do not be dismayed, for the LORD your God is with you wherever you go.

We all know that it is far too easy to go through the motions of life and be consumed with whatever is coming at us on any given day. Sometimes we just simply compartmentalize our time with God and our time doing "life." What if there was a different way to think about it? God truly is with you all the time and everywhere you go.

Whether or not you are aware of our Father's presence, He is there.

Pause.

That is really amazing! Maybe even a little frightening. He is always with us. At work, at home, even on vacation.

One of my favorite places to go, where I find I am more keenly aware of his presence, is the beach. There is something about the vast ocean in front of me, the sound of waves crashing, the breeze in my face, the creatures that I can see—and those that I can't—that I am just in awe of. We live in such a beautiful world that he created for us. Yet not only did he create it, he is present among us. Where is your favorite place to go to feel Him near you?

Be purposeful about spending quiet time with Him so that you can hear His voice, but also practice existing in the awareness that your Father is with you, even when you are cooking dinner or washing the dishes. Sometimes all it takes is a nod and a wink to acknowledge and be aware that He is with you always.

Reflection: Reflect about the times that you have been aware of His presence. How might you encourage that awareness at other times?

Action: Give thanks that He loves you so much that He always wants to spend time with you. His grace, His strength, His love in all things. Beautiful.

2 Corinthians 12:9 – And He said to me, "My grace is sufficient for you, for My strength is made perfect in weakness." Therefore most gladly I will rather boast in my infirmities, that the power of Christ may rest upon me.

Romans 8:38-39 – For I am persuaded that neither death nor life, nor angels nor principalities nor powers, nor things present nor things to come, nor height nor depth, nor any other created thing, shall be able to separate us from the love of God which is in Christ Jesus our Lord.

Thought-Provoking and Encouraging Messages

1) God wants the best for you.

2) You always have a choice. Be intentional.

3) Be curious and not judgmental.

4) Live in the moment. Yesterday is in the past, and tomorrow has yet to be written.

5) You are perfectly created the way that you are.

6) Never quit. Hold on to Hope.

7) Be relentless and run your race with endurance.

8) Jesus at the center makes all things possible.

9) Believe in His ALL and His everything.

10) Correction and condemnation are not the same thing. One is out of love, the other is not.

11) Do not fight against what you cannot change.

12) Life is a series of marathons. Embrace each one.

13) Seek to find the best in others.

14) Be the light and love others, even when they may not deserve it. Jesus gave it to you first.

*15) **Remember the footsteps. In times of trial, there is only one set, and they are not yours.***

16) Do not hold on to worries, for even a glass of water becomes too heavy if you hold on.

17) Be a duck. Let it roll down your back.

18) Believe. When God says "always" and "in all things," He means just that.

19) There is beauty all around you. Open your eyes and see.

20) Learn from Peter. With Jesus on your boat, you will not sink.

21) God will be part of your story, whether or not you invite Him.

Scripture Reference

Psalm 34:18
Matthew 5:4
Deuteronomy 31:6
Psalm 46:10
Psalm 56:8
Isaiah 41:10
Philippians 4:19
Philippians 4:13
Joshua 1:9
Psalm 147:3
Matthew 11:28
2 Corinthians 1:3
Proverbs 10:7
John 3:16
Psalm 112:6
Proverbs 17:17
Galatians 6:2
Ecclesiastes 4:9-12
Romans 8:18
John 16:22
Revelation 21:4
Hebrews 4:16
John 20:29
Romans 5:1-5
Joshua 1:9
Psalm 29:11

Deuteronomy 31:8
Romans 12:2
Philippians 4:7
Hebrews 4:15,16
Psalm 4:8
Jeremiah 31:25
Matthew 11:28-30
Matthew 22:37-40
John 15:12-13
Romans 12:10
Ephesians 2:10
Romans 12:13
Proverbs 11:25
1 John 4:16
1 John 4:9-11
John 15:13
John 14:2
John 16:33
1 Thessalonians 4:13-14
2 Corinthians 5:7
Matthew 19:26
James 2:18
John 16:22
John 15:11
Philippians 4:7
Proverbs 3:5-6
Matthew 6:34
Romans 8:28
Proverbs 2:6-8
Psalm 9:1
Matthew 6:33
Psalm 144:1
Revelation 3:20
Psalm 31:7
Joshua 1:9
2 Corinthians 12:9
Romans 8:38-39

About the Author

Adam is a devoted, grateful, husband and father with over 35 years experience in healthcare. After co-authoring several articles published in various healthcare journals, this is his first solo publication outside that arena.

He enjoys traveling, dining where the "locals" eat, serving at church, running and playing an occasional round of golf. Most of all, he receives immense pleasure out of spending quality time with family and friends. Life is best when done together.